ELEPHANT STREET

ELEPHANT STREET

RON CHARACH

George Amabile, Editor

Acknowledgments
The author wishes to thank series editor George Amabile, and poets Susan Ioannou and Andy Patton for helpful suggestions at varying stages in the development of the manuscript. The poem "The Night After" is dedicated to Dr. Susan Goldberg.

The poems "In Panic as Killers Close in" and "Jerusalem Earthquake" contain direct quotes from press articles by Martin Regg Cohn and Khaled Abu Toameh, respectively. The italicized quote that ends "A Fateful Rendering" was written by Andy Patton in honour of Joseph Brodsky. Italicized lines in the poem "Elephant Street" are quoted, with permission, from *Gates of Prayer: The New Union Prayer Book*, copyright 1975 by the Central Conference of American Rabbis.

Several of these poems first appeared in *CV II, Descant, Matrix, The Medical Post, The New Quarterly* and *Prism International*. "Five-pattern Baldness" will appear in the anthology *Body Language: Head to Toe*, Black Moss Press.

Cover design by Terry Gallagher/Doowah Design.
Cover photo, "Victory at Queen," by Ron Charach.
Photo of Ron Charach by Irving Posluns.

This book was printed on Ancient Forest Friendly paper.
Printed and bound in Canada by AGMV Marquis Imprimeur Inc.

We acknowledge the support of The Canada Council for the Arts and the Manitoba Arts Council for our publishing program.

National Library of Canada Cataloguing in Publication Data

Charach, Ron
     Elephant Street / Ron Charach

Poems.
ISBN 0-921833-89-X

     I. Title.

PS8555.H39834E43 2003   C811'.54   C2003-910201-7
PR9199.3.C4727E43 2003

Signature Editions, P.O. Box 206, RPO Corydon, Winnipeg, Manitoba, R3M 3S7

for my brother Arthur

ELEPHANT STREET

Prologue:
Omniscient Narrator   11

Safe Passage
A Daughter's Dance   15
Charades   16
Trim   17
Safe Passage   18
Circle Barbecue   20
Corporate Tonto   21
In Late-Arriving Winter   22
The Nightly News   23
Cottage Clean   24
Houses at Night   25
Festive   26

Painted Figures
At the Resort   29
Bully   31
"Have You Seen This Man?   33
Blindness   34
"The Dustman or The Lovers"   35
"Love Among the Nations"   37
Wandering Styrofoam   39
Painted Figures   41

Inside this Screen, My Body
"In Panic as Killers Close In…"   45
Jerusalem Earthquake   47
Inside This Screen, My Body   48
Food (Fad)   49
Uneasy on the Open Field   51
Missing and Presumed   52
We Kill the Afternoon   53
The Cage Dweller   54
There Is a Familiarity   55
Tombstone Flicker   56
Two Walks, Same Night   57

The Consultant

Five-Pattern Baldness   61
Endocrinology   63
Man in a Pinstripe Mood   64
The Humming Fire Hall   66
Tammy Wynette   67
Harlequins   68
Last Call   69
The Old Cardiology Dream   70
Buttons Sleeping   71

Elephant Street

A Fateful Rendering   75
Temporary Power   76
Paint-Can Hero   77
The Foley Artist   78
Riffs on Dignity   80
Blue Sperm Whale   81
Elephant Street   83

Epilogue:

At The Roanoke   87
The Night After   90

PROLOGUE

OMNISCIENT NARRATOR

This is a morning for the books.

Along the air terminal corridor,
a svelte blonde is pulled by two Dobermans,
while far away on both coasts, some man in a diner
is served his coffee first because
he is, or is not, aboriginal.

Behind me, in the security lineup, someone is thinking
Had I skipped work, I could have done my accents for the kids:
the Servisol workman or the Jamaican carpenter in dreads
who'll come to nail the half-inch plywood over
the spot where Jonah whacked his tennis ball
straight through the drywall. I turn towards him,
try not to offer too knowing a smile.

Not like the psychologist doddering on ahead
muttering under her breath
after a long day trying to stay
two pages in the manual ahead of her patients.
There will be no delays, much less a strip search.
They might have swabbed the underside of my shoe,
but the spectrometer calibration is off today.
Though not by much.

Boarding, my step need not be cautious.
My bag carries a fat classic I know all too well,
along with my battery-powered *vade mecums*.
(I know when each is set to expire.)
The flight attendant smiles as she greets me
and points out my assigned seat, unsuspecting.
How lively she looks for one who was packing
at 5:00 A.M. for a 7:30 flight.
I consider her brass wings outspread,
her rehearsal for the security spiel
and her thoughts about the bulge
in the first officer's pants
before he and the captain disappeared behind the curtain.
I feel no need to penetrate to where the principals sit.
Omniscient narrator of this ponderous adult production,
I declare they both looked confident and rested.
Otherwise, I don't know what I'd do.

SAFE PASSAGE

A DAUGHTER'S DANCE

As a baby, you squirmed in vain to loosen
pink plastic orthopedic shoes.
Now on the family room Persian rug,
you improvise jazz ballet
to your favourite tape, *A Gift from Israel.*
The martial slant of these proud songs
bounces off you, still young enough
to dance without a top, yet you've grown
to play Martha Graham in your class's "Night of the Notables."
Wasn't it yesterday I helped you clamber aboard the trampoline
while Mommy sewed your witch's suit?
As a toddler, when I left you in the bathroom,
"Okay, Doll, I'll give you your privacy,"
you protested, "I want *Mommy* to give me my privacy!"

One day, you'll get it from us both,
so much, you and your brother won't know
what to make of where we disappeared.
Like me, you are wary of a long night
spent in an empty house, though my advice is
turn those blind corners quickly,
keep your tummy tight as a drum,
and thank the gods of exposure training
for a rich imagination.

Of course, there is unfinished business,
that plea for a dog we keep putting off.
Lately it's a border collie
we're too stressed to walk, too reluctant to board
when away on trips, but perhaps
we're overly fond of our carpets.
What else to expect from a man with a bad back
doing stretches on the floor, and wanting neither
his circles interrupted nor his face licked,
who sleeps so lightly that heaven itself
tiptoes around his dreams?

Like your brother, you are on loan to us, as we are to you.
If we do break down and get that little dog
it won't be from surrendering to
the pull of your unfathomable dance.

CHARADES

We clear the living room for charades.
New to the game,
I'm assigned to the children's team:
six-year-old Charlotte
instructs me on symbols
for "a," "the," "movie," "TV program," "book,"
also "man," "woman," "thing,"
and Clara cooks us a winner:
"international space station."

Promoted to the adult team
teenaged Phoebe, to our delight,
writhes and explodes
guess after guess, as the adults veer
ever-so-slightly off the mark

until they regroup, and nearly solve us—
with "the human genome project."
Dorothy's "sounds like" clues,
take us close as "ooman jeansome projeck,"
our reward the clock stopped
by Clara's father Doug.
"Ooman jeansome projeck?" we repeat,
as they laugh off our hollow victory:
"The human genome project!"

After the game, bright-eyed Amelia
asks her physicist uncle,
"What's the human genome project?"
and slightly cocks her ten-year-old blonde head
as if ready for our avid,
if overqualified, timekeeper
to take all the time he needs.

TRIM

He steps up first
to the chair and clipper,

the square-jawed fifty-year-old
with longish salt 'n pepper hair and matching beard
and makes pained conversation as she snips
through handful after handful of his former life.

When his chin is clean, she slips his specs back on
and holds up the glass that tells no lies.
He starts at how much of his face is showing,
lowers his brow, resists a double take,
and fumbles for his wallet,
reckoning the exchange:

barer, slighter—younger.
Sails trimmed.

SAFE PASSAGE
Glenn Gould versus Gordie Howe

At thirty-five going on fifty,
his library is a forest of self-help books
where he seeks shelter and knows
M. Scott Peck from Anthony Robbins,
Deepak Chopra from every other
guru for landlubbers on life's storm-swept deck.

Brother to all who creep with tripwire nerves,
sandlot chickens who duck the line drive,
white-tailed deer of the office party...
At the beach a blanket covers his chalky legs
and on the high-swaying pier that succumbs to the freeze
and needs to be rebuilt each spring,
he clutches white-knuckled at the railing.
Weak in the knees, he crawls back on all fours,
his five-year-old egging him on, *"Oh, Daaa-ddy!"*

Pregnant women unsettle him,
as do the still-forming bones of newborns,
or the racket at construction sites—even
hidden behind high green plywood walls.
Think of crushable toes in a work boot
jangling like a tinful that *isn't* stones.
Oily workmen's gloves careening from girders
make him draw in his ribs for that dizzying
pool of air leased to "real" *and* nervous men.

If only his wife were half as harried.
Unwavering, she draws up lists, files recipes,
(every woman an authority on the man
she could have/should have married.)
He trusts only a lady barber, ears twitching
even to delicately wielded shears.
In his youth he listened by moonlit radio
while a female doctor explained the fickle bodies of the sexes.

As a kid in the sprawling men's room of the stadium
needing to pee at the crowded intermission,
a hundred adult peckers lolling over the trough
made him forget how to initiate,
though he'd stored enough for his bladder to burst.
Better suited, as an adult, for more private performances,

like using a popsicle stick and a wipe down
to clean dog-dirt from his daughter's sneakers
on a soothing green suburban lawn.

Even in humid summer his car windows stay shut
to guard the air-conditioned space from vengeful hornets
whose appetites switch by mid-July
from flower pollen to human sugars,
while his own family buzzes around his head:
the turn he should have made, that extra pick-up
he ought to try, just once: "It's the slow drivers, Dad,
that cause accidents."
"God forbid, accidents," knee-jerk he murmurs,
easing his crash-rated automobile
beneath the shelter of the car park
with the child-friendly basketball hoop.

>   Oh to cruise the manly ice
>   like that old farmhand Gordie Howe,
>   to stick-handle past the foe
>   but when cornered, elbow a nose or a jaw.

>   Once when Mark Howe got decked,
>   Gordie skated behind the foolhardy forward
>   still pummeling his boy
>   and pulled the man to his feet— *by the nostrils*—

>   Better the trance of nervous dormancy,
>   Glenn Gould in the studio humming up a sweat
>   over the *Goldberg Variations*, and never
>   returning to live performance,
>   though many predicted he would.

You, limo driver, who navigates
the stations of the city's airport roads,
be patient if you spy him in your mirror
frowning at the traffic, the pollution and the noise.

Raise the brim of your chauffeur's hat
from your eyes and marvel at the Absolution:
a hard, winding canyon of a world
that, for now, allows even a man like this
safe passage.

CIRCLE BARBECUE

Three years running, Tom hauls his propane barbecue
onto the grassy circle between our three streets.
Everyone is invited to bring
kids and desserts and drinks and folding chairs
for a cottage chat in the middle of the big city.
Some cancel other events not to miss it.

There's talk about the Conservatives,
their promise to eliminate "bureaucrats"
—obviously toothless fish-eyed hunchbacks in wigs
who scratch their names on dusty forms
behind thick doors of bevelled glass.
They've come up with a "common sense revolution":
Why can't stay-at-home welfare moms
look after the children of working welfare moms?
These Tories detest everything about our city,
and spurn its role as the engine of the economy.

Chatting over dinosaur paper plates and plastic forks
beneath a clear sky, you avoid asking
any you don't know well what it is they *do,*
not wanting to hear about fruitless job searches
or contract work for lousy pay,
or department store salesmen stretched to cover
toys and cameras and luggage at the same time
while irate customers clamour for service.
Many have resigned, sadly agreeing
to be bought out for their benefits.
Pouring beer into a tall plastic cup, you remember
this nation once was rich in good, secure jobs.
When did it change? When did the entrepreneur
overtake the minister, the scientist and the physician
as a figure for youthful adulation?

Ah, but this is the circle barbecue,
and even if some yahoo premier Out West
is galloping eastward, waving
his scythe at weaklings, no-hopers and socialists,
meadow quarry, we bite into a long hot dog, twist open a cool one
with the hopeless cheer of free citizens
determined as our young to enjoy a summer's day
whether or not bean-counting horsemen
are on their way.

CORPORATE TONTO

After the last manager has left for his suburb
—once they were called vice presidents
and were interpreters:
"Don't take what you do here personally.
 Remember, you're a salaried employee;
 you don't get to eat what you kill."
he collapses at the triangle desk that supports his computer,
aching brow across folded arms,
red blotch on the forehead.
With thumb and forefinger he grasps his pegged front tooth:
still no wiggle; a mercy.
Then the carpal-tunnel tingle
creeps across the backs of his hands
as he tries to rid his mind of an image:
the happy hunting grounds
as a company picnic, with oral presentations.

> *TV Tonto Jay Silver Heels,*
> *a Six Nation Mohawk from Ontario,*
> *would say things on the horse opera in mock-Indian*
> *that were malaprops and lampoons.*

Like a trusty scout, he listens.
Thin formica registers faint rumblings
from the maze of double glass doors.
The hum of the water cooler,
the blue buzz of fluorescents
mask a furtive tread in the hallway:
a *kemo sabe* returning for his umbrella, for take-home work?
Or the determined gait of the well-insured,
striding in gleaming tassled shoes,
girded with the hide of a steer,
the wool of a sheep, coming closer
like a living death tax,
—coming after his little red
benefits.

IN LATE-ARRIVING WINTER

In the winter that nearly wasn't,
a surprising December sun
lures the mercury skyward by fifteen degrees.
The homeless are granted a reprieve,
and the ungloved at food banks have time
to sort through bins of bruised vegetables
and hunt for novel varieties of macaroni shell,
new flavours of canned soup.

I attend an artist friend's show called "Cancelled"
(a hard show to advertise)
and covet a four-piece installation titled *Swamped.*
Two golden-tinted blow-ups of submerged trees
flank bright floral paintings that mirror each other.
Across the photos of swamp, Bergmannesque,
she has lettered quotations,
both favourable and damning,
from critics of her past work.
One reads: "A dull sociological stew."
I have to laugh at that one, thinking, *Just like a political poem…*
Later I tell the artist, "It's hard to believe
how the price of art keeps climbing when there's no market."

Or that sudden slashes to welfare
will drive more poor into the streets
with or without their young. There they are!
never thinking to look up at our high windows.
There is no snow yet
to background their furious plight.
But who are we fooling by postponing
the weather by a week or two?
Ours has always been a wintry place,
a cold uneasy peace.

THE NIGHTLY NEWS

Tonight, visiting Florida from Canada,
the young father, nursing a winter cold,
watches the news with muted sound,
stifling a cough so his children,
a few feet away, just the other side
of an accordion-door,
can sleep.

Stirring in blue-beamed darkness: the conscience,
unyielding as one of those bulbous ceramic
end-table lamps from the Fifties,
a separate chain hanging from each compartment.
Under my shade, it proclaims,
are the blinding secrets
of the hemispheres...

"Forget fancy-shmancy furniture and *shmatahs*."
The silver-haired grandpa from Russia-via-Brooklyn
joins his son-in-law, now that his *aynickles* are in bed.
"You spend time with your lovely family;
let others piss away their lives
on fast cars and sailboats.
Remember, even Kennedys and Rockefellers
eventually come 'round;
A generation of thieves is followed
by a generation who can afford
to be philanthropists."

In silence, on the night screen
they witness other families struggle,
women with shrunken breasts nursing unconsolable babies
palming unclean water, performing
the slow unsanctified rituals
of the poor.

At sunrise two children punch-drunk on light
pull grandpa's bathrobe from a frayed wicker chair,
belly-flop on the waterbed and scream their good fortune.

COTTAGE CLEAN

At the cottage
even a sweaty T-shirt will do
for another day at the beach,
and in the kitchen, a chipped floor tile,
its gummy-backed grip loosened by blasts from a hair dryer,
can be lifted with the cheese slicer.
So what if the bathroom floor around the tub
is soft and houses earwigs,
if the old log chairs with hand-fitted joints
now have more nails in them than wood.
For the young ones a good day
is beach volleyball, a swim and repainting the welcome sign.

Beachside, the conversations.
"You have grown children?" I ask.
"Well…" Her eyes mist over.
She tells of a lively older son
who played the troll under the bridge
to delight visiting children, but whom she lost
to low-hanging fog, freshly tinted car windows,
a "country stop" at an intersection,
and another young man's van,
Rottweiler in the back seat
and no chance to swerve.

"Usually I can talk about it just fine,
but here, every 'keeper' Josh ever caught stirs up memory."
We smooth things over with talk of cottage foundations
(hers is concrete block, while ours 'floats' on bricks and two-by-fours.)
The kids, getting way too much sun,
look all the healthier for it.

On this sacred ground,
even the rules of science show mercy,
at least off the highway, on resort land
where heavy mists, rising from the lake
soften the asphalt's cleanly marked lanes,
as determined cars haul canoes on trailers,
all the usual escapes…

HOUSES AT NIGHT

On the lush ravine side of Strathearn Circle
haze and mystery cloak the mansions
until in one, the lights switch on
and leaded windows reveal
blonde panelling topped with wallpaper brocade
and hanging over the mantle a bountiful landscape
titled something like *Pleasures of the Hunt,*
on either side a blue-green trellis
each with its golden-orange peacock.

An inner Mr. Hyde would propel me up the flagstone hill
to tear away the English ivy
and slam the Medusa knocker,
rattling the bevelled glass beneath
its wrought-iron *fleur-de-lis* grillework
—until it shatters,
jarring her from her bedroom talk-show
and from his perch at the circular bar
the master who, I swear, on the Sabbath eve
rubbed his pool cue across his fly and cursed
missing a banked shot "by a cunt-hair"
within his daughter's hearing.

—The same who now tosses back auburn hair
as she strides up the stairway, to where
tradition meets renovation, "The Addition"
with twice the breathing space of the original home,
five times its parlour ration
in a temple that houses but four souls
who all can shower at the same time.
She wears the confident glow of a latter-born
on her way to bath
without so much as a nod
for the Impressionists on the landing
or a need to see into the envious night
or contemplate her family's fortune, purring-smooth
as the high-tech razor caressing her legs in the mist.

Astride a bidet, or stepping back into her kimono,
she may sense the itch of a slight imperfection,
the fatigue from too long a day in the sun,
yet how adorable, her iconic reflection
in the wet marble tile, unweeping.

FESTIVE

In his *oeuvre*, every poet wants a festive poem.
Who knows when he might be called upon
to top the misrhyming doggerel that celebrates
each member of the office and their *raison d'être?*

In *this* poem the decorations hold fast
the pink and gold balloons bob in place,
not a bauble breaks, no clown snarls,
and the punch is never salted with tears.

The freshly deceased are kept at bay.
Workmates taking time off for health reasons
are exceptions to the rule that life, like work, paddles on
with a smooth and efficient stroke.

May ours be a happy and prosperous New Year
(only a whinger need add healthy.)
May we meet again twelve months from now,
having grown (but not fatter) with the company.

May we wear the scowling eyes
and smirking nose of W.C. Fields
whose greeting was "Happy Holidays
to all my friends except two."

PAINTED FIGURES

AT THE RESORT

Muscular, mustachioed, our guide Carlos fills us in.
On economics:
"Wee drivers do no get a reel wage per ow-er,
and so you most geev teeps."
On racism:
"There eez no soch theeng in Mehico,
We are all 40% Spaneesh, 40% from thee Eendian, and 20% Black.
We are all called Gonzalez.
You weel note how we all have black hair,
but no on our chest or our arm."
On bargaining:
"Jost re-member, you hwan' to buy, and dhey hwan' to sell.
Dhere eez only hwone problem: *el ultimo precio.*"
On population density:
"Een North Amereeca you hwan' a relayteev
who eez a doctor or a lawhyer.
Here een Mehico we all hwan'
a relative who eez een constroction,
who can beeld thee extra room for thee new *bebe*
an' thee Gaudelajara cozzin veezeeting from Yooniversity
an' thee cozzin who has move een and weel stay
teel she eez old enoff to mahrry."

Can we guess what this Carlos is thinking,
any more than the restaurant Captain,
compact, chisel-featured, more than 40% Indian,
who serves us with begrudging dignity
Spanish and Mexican coffees,
risking the burn ward nightly as he pours
blue flames back and forth from one metal vessel to another.

Or the equally Indian man and his wife
who dole out towels to *turistas* without pockets
who wouldn't think to pay at an "all-inclusive"
for such a throw-away service
as a politely proffered towel or its signed-off return.

As for tipping, our new Alberta friend Garnet,
lounge lizard, strictly CEO material,
hauls us at midnight to hear a gifted classical guitarist
whom he tips with only an enthusiastic ear.

Hospital-style, we wear the resort's blue bands
that interfere with sex play, but grant
us the right to march up to any bar
and order in the Spanish of Texans
and a few adventurous Canadians, *una cerveza, una* tequila sunrise,
una Margarita, por favor, como los otros.

Black-haired Carina, *Actividad* Staff, her long chocolate-brown limbs
and boundless energy in a blue bikini,
could get your granny to play water polo.
She steps high in the nightly Vegas-style shows.
Remember her like those sunsets on the Bay of Banderas,
where Cortez and his almighty horses drew up short
at the sight of banners of red, green and gold—eclipsed
by the gleam of his armour, as the sky
recruited band after band of cloud
into a show of unnatural red.

BULLY

Sprawled on a deck chair, eyeing the kids,
he clouds my stay at this sunny resort.
Under a crest of spiked dirty blond hair,
he is the red-faced, thick-necked interloper,
a disgruntled young adult yet to score
a job taking apart escalators, or breathing acetone fumes.
His lip curls as he considers our family leisure,
mulls over my soft blue Italian leather pouch
and declares himself, through a long glare,
ready to realize my worst fears.

For a moment a lovely daughter in a green bikini
flashes before me, my dearest, barest part.
No time to ask, "Where would *I* be without hatred?"
Instead, I keep the children under close watch,
ring the hotel manager, the police—pidgin English and all—
marshal five hundred years of British law.
Do we cut our stay short?
Take drastic action?
I review my own list of victims:

> That other ancient people
> whose youth forfeit their humanity
> by wiring themselves to bombs;

> that bedside neurosurgeon
> in full hearing of the patient,
> who questioned us, "Is this man demented?
> Would you hire him as an accountant?"
> As he left those poor eyes gazing into space,
> he proclaimed, "I wouldn't let this man rake my leaves."

> Those immigrant Hebrew teachers,
> with accents as dated as their wide-lapel suits.
> Among them, Mr. Sari
> who in all Diaspora weather
> wore a Salvation Army greatcoat
> and who our class stunned by bringing in
> an identical four or five
> to hang beside his own
> in the roomy teacher's closet.

That fidgety, lonesome Kenneth Trachnik
at the boys' camp I attended on bursary,
about whom I sang *sotto voce* in a friendship circle,
"Kenneth T. is very gay,
Hey-lawdy, lawdy-lo
. . . Sits on the toilet night and day-ay,
Hey lawdy, lawdy-lo. . ."
as the girls and boys laughed
at the new camp jester's quarry
and a squirming Kenneth took off
—for the toilets!
as my counsellor shot me a look of concern.

But this young bully has sticks and stones
and on a day bright with possibility,
the sea as tranquil as a papered-over past,
scrawls on the back of my bar receipt
more than payback to me and mine:
DIRTY FRIENDLY SMILEY KIKE.

"Have You Seen This Man?
Missing Since May 13, 2002"

Overnight, outside my office
on the street the signs mushroom,
in large block letters the word "Reward",
with "offered by family" neatly penned in
above a colour photo of a man too vibrant to stay in focus.
In red, his name "Dr. Mitchel Wineberg,
psychiatrist, age 37."

"Last seen Spadina and Bloor
White male, 5'8", 170 lbs., medium build
May go by the name Pooch or Poochy
May be wandering disoriented with the homeless.
Feared at risk of suicide."

Mornings later, the dreaded obituary
mentions patients and the homeless
to whom the doctor was especially kind
missing him, along with his dog Farfel,
a curiously personal detail, the name
a man chooses for the family pet.

Once the circulars spring up,
it is usually too late, the old downward spiral
of discontinuity: psychiatrist, lost soul, missing person.
The shapes in which a man roams the earth
leave a legacy of mushrooming clichés:
How tragic, So young a man,
There but for the grace of God go I…
less the stuff of bulletin than religious bumper sticker
complete with slogan,
"Far From God? Who Moved?"
and perhaps a computer-generated icon,
the face of a tortured, long-absent prophet,
"Have You Seen This Man?"

BLINDNESS

On a ravine walk, Buttons and I
meet Katherine in dark glasses, led by her two dogs
Lucy and Cassandra, too easily lured
by other canines from their guide duties.

I take the plunge. "Pardon my asking,
but were you ever sighted?"

"Not since I was a year old," her British accent replies.
"Congenital glaucoma
left a real mess inside with the scarring,
but I can still see lightning.
As a child I was intrigued by flashlights,
and my brothers used magnifying glasses
to catch me the sun's rays.
I could have corneal transplants,
but I might lose the little light I have.
'But that's *useless* anyway,' the doctor said.
'Not to *me*, it isn't.'
It's amazing the things people say.
Just the other day an elderly woman asked me,
'Does your mother know where you are?'
'Oh,' I told her, 'I *always*
tell my mother *everything*.'
She caught my drift."

"Have you heard," I ask her, "of the novel
by Nobel Prize-winner José Saramago
about an epidemic of *contagious* blindness
and how it unravels a city's social fabric
—it's a powerful allegory—more depressing than uplifting.
But afterwards, you never again take sight for granted."

"I'm not sure," she says, "that I need such a book these days."

As we part, I recall a recent interview
with Saramago, who, in an old Iberian moment,
compared to Auschwitz an Israeli incursion
into the West Bank town of Ramallah.
But is there a place for the blindness of visionaries
in a chance meeting, on an evening of snowdrifts
bright with moonlight?

"THE DUSTMAN OR THE LOVERS"

Foreshadowing his exit from the Royal Academy,
at the centre of Stanley Spencer's great cartoon painting of 1934,
a towering figure in Christ-white skirt and pink polka-dot blouse
hoists her bald little dustman like an icon into the air,
exulting in his trouser legs wrapped around her.
Like stymied interpreters, husbands/labourers
and matrons in stiffly formal perms, arms akimbo,
look on, impatient with the spectacle,
even as two offer up strange homely gifts.
From Spencer: "Nothing I love is rubbish
and so I resurrect the teapot, and the empty jam tin and the cabbage stalks,
and as there is a mystery in the Trinity, so there is in these three
and many others of no apparent significance."

On a World Socialist Web site,
looking back from 2000, Paul Mitchell writes:
"The joy of his bliss is spiritual in his union with his wife
who carries him in her arms and experiences the bliss of union
with his corduroy trousers… they are gazed at by other reuniting
wives of old labourers."
But who *are* these male witnesses?
One, bare-chested in overalls, and dumbfounded,
could well be the dustman's assistant.
He too is wearing work boots,
while standing behind him, dispassionate,
is an elderly man in a white beard.
I try to square a white picket fence
with the topiary peacock and spiral hedges strategically placed
to halo the bald dustman, and mistake him for
a plump middle-aged woman with hedgerow hair.
I feel for another small bearded figure in the background
who needs to look away from this broad-daylight confusion.

Sniffed the Royal Academy: One rejects
such "distortions and peculiarity."

Rear-left, there stands at attention a unisex figure
in an Eastern-looking floral robe,
while, in the foreground, asleep on a small patch of lawn,
lolls a panther-sized white tabby.
Is this worth waking up to: the Adoration of The Dustman
by working-class and middle-class magi?
To me, the scarecrow-straw corduroys

invoke a Christ-like John Barleycorn,
elevated to his rightful place by a gray-haired unkempt Mary.
Glorious ambiguity, "The Dustman or The Lovers"—which is it?
Yet, this artist painted perfectly real onions
in "Greenhouse and Garden", and many noble portraits
even bitch-goddess Vera Similitude would smile upon
though in a light less unabashedly bright
than that day in Stanley Spencer's Cookham
where a lowly dustman rose
heavenward, enraptured—surprised!—
by the great mystery
of modernity.

"LOVE AMONG THE NATIONS"

In the Stanley Spencer oil, 1935,
two gray-haired British matrons preside in the far margins,
one bends a Turk's head towards her bosom
to adore the tassel hanging from his fez,

On the right, uneasy, a granny submits to
groping by two loving African men,
one wearing not a stitch
stands behind her billowy white dress,
while the second palms her privates, an elongated leg
stretching from his loin cloth like a fifth limb.

Startled, off-center, a tweedy Spencer-like chap
is undressed by a gentle African in a crepe skirt
and his female companion, lusciously naked
but for hula-hoops of bone, her partly shaven head
topped by brown clumps of matted hair.
Meanwhile, a male Chinese, fully clothed,
serene beneath wide-spreading coolie hat
sports a boutonnière of poppies that seem to swoon
at the touch of *his* African paramour.

In the foreground, a well-dressed British matron
with her anklets-wearing African man
caresses his muscular leg and each individual toe.
Draped in black nuns' habits,
featureless mummies with chimney-like headdresses
approach and withdraw from two reticent young British men,
who, again, are fully, even overly, clothed.

　　　At the center, in contrast,
an African man and woman share a relaxed moment
— she in more Western dress, except for a large ring of bone through her nose.

Waiting in the dimly lit rear
of a large pavilion, African women
bulge pregnant bellies, or carry young babes.
A small Black girl takes the arm, and accepts the hand
of two naked White children,
the only bare members of the British Isles
in this surreal display that a senior Anglican critic
praised as infused with the love of humanity.

What to make of Stanley Spencer,
advocate of world peace through free love,
who painted his bisexual second wife with a carnal flourish
of pendulous breasts and blue veins showing through translucent skin;
who bequeathed, among his many works,
"Sunflower and Dog Worship" and "Adoration of the Old Men,"
"works," one critic said, "in which sex is treated too oddly
to be collected much outside his native Britain."

"Love Among the Nations" exudes a magisterial strangeness.
Should our eyes be distracted or bemused
by this brave new world, where love is inexorable as tribal hatred,
whether draftily free in Hottentot attire, or stiffly formal in Harris tweeds,
or even in the deathly black raiment of surreal nuns
who either accept a man, or lean away when he draws near.
Has British reserve ever been so tested, importuned,
so gently or so weirdly breached
—all in the service of a cosmic cartoon portrait
of ancestral strivings that might finally yield that chimera,
the truly global human.

WANDERING STYROFOAM

As I kick through snowdrifts on the journey home,
the Styrofoam bowl-with-lid retains the heat
of my vegetable soup à la Magritte,
a spicy broth of carrot, potato, orange and leek,
with long wisps of dill
like eyelashes from a Dali.

I said home, though my office is *mon vrai destin*,
a home-away-from-home
with baronial brick arches and stone façade
fronting lush wall-to-wall
that hugs the beige corridors
hung with original art *partout*.

This new *Francophonie* is one effect
of ordering such a soup.

I regret that in my emergency store
Spanish is *poco poco*
and I could not exclaim
à la Goya, Velasquez or Picasso
even had their signatures swum into view
after the long slow ladle stir.

In the wintry air, my tightly-tied package swings
in its translucent bag;
I hope to arrive with it seething still
and escape the cold fate of a *vichyssoise*.
I need to be warmed from the inside,
the way my dog feels when I compliment her,
the way it is when my slender masseuse
suggests I slip out of my boxer shorts
"to improve access," and settles my body
into an hour and a half of heaven.

In the bitter wind, my gloves clasp Styrofoam.
How easy, to crush its genius
that retains the impact of the cauldron,
and of Mark Strand, who defends
our right to lunch on lyric poems
even as the fires of Holocaust
smoulder in the ruins of Ground Zero.

I'm almost there, cradling my prize
to deliverance into its new warm home,
the plush pink alimentary canal,
and try not to think of other vessels
that preserved the warmth of blood,
—*Kindertransport.*
What kind of term is that
for a punctual professional
noon-hour-vegetarian
representational
North American
Jew—

PAINTED FIGURES

I might have been painted into "The Happy Accidents of the Swing" by Fragonard, in which mademoiselle's slipper flies off, to the great delight of her lordly beau and curious onlooking cupids in stone; or Constable's "The Cornfield" where a country lad lies prostrate before a cool woodland stream. Instead I popped up in the last century.

Cows have been fed the brains of other cows: a Stalingrad of animals set alight, the distant Smoking Mountains of the prematurely slaughtered. And somewhere else, bored with anthrax, Saddam Hussein perhaps dreams of dropping infected goats like bombs spreading another virus on moist winds, contagious as an evangelical religion.

The modern canvas is seamless, endless. A great desert, without brushstroke— and no carrion; scavengers have gobbled up every morsel. No evidence of birds. They've all vanished into some old song no one remembers.

I wish I could find a good book in which to make my home. But I'll have to stretch this canvas, with pliers and staple gun, make my paints from the tar pool that has oozed up through the twentieth century's landfill.

What can I render? A hearty scream from the hairless mouth of Modernism, Bacon's Pope Innocent the Tenth beaming death rays from an electrified throne, painted to strains of Beethoven transformed into a high-pitched tune on a cell phone?

Or a shapely Gothic vamp with implanted lips and breasts prancing in black leather through a movie based on a video game? Is a conference call to Lucas or Spielberg in order, after nothing new arrives and the brushes are left soaking and the mind lusts for a mission compelling as Rembrandt scouring the ghetto for the faces of nobility?

INSIDE THIS SCREEN, MY BODY

"IN PANIC AS KILLERS CLOSE IN..."

I write this tonight because for the past six weeks,
using scalpel blade and alcohol,
moleskin and scotch tape,
I have been shaving at the base
of my son's plantar warts,
a wincing act of care
that skirts the base of cruelty

and because, in this morning's *Star,*
of a photo titled LOST HOPE.
Sleepless haunted eyes
festooned by windblown hair,
Algerian Assia Bayeesh looks out at the reader,
holding a tiny girl who pulls at her sleeve, revealing
a stretch of lacy cotton.
"Assia Bayeesh, 18, clutches a girl
pulled from a terrorist's fire in Sidi Rais.
The cousin who saved the girl was killed for the act."

Who is taking young women as sex slaves
in *zawaj al mutaa,* "marriages of pleasure"
that strip the jewels from their victims?

Who is hurling babies from rooftops
into makeshift bonfires
while chanting "God is great!"
—*Mujahideen?*

Who is slitting villagers' throats
or, as they themselves plead,
Qui tué qui?

The Armed Islamic Group?
The army? Local thugs
the army uses
to justify its presence?

They know too well who *it* is.

Nor are we all innocence.
As teens, my friends and I had our "cruelty index"
that licensed jokes at the expense of the infirm
(careful not to be overheard)

forgetting that our own people
wandered the earth in black
receiving a gypsy's welcome.

I write this tonight to forgo
my people's monopoly on holocaust,
to say that again and again the world stares up
at the leering mustachioed face of massacre:
Germany, Russia, Poland,
Armenia, Bosnia, Cambodia—Rwanda!
Iraq versus Iran, with keys to heaven issued
to the first wave of teenagers to rush the enemy howitzers;
the take-no-prisoners Nintendo wars of Uncle Sam.
Tonight it burns in some far-off desert land
that expat Canadians have fled
to sleep in their embassy's beds.

Tonight I want my country
to admit no fanatics, torturers, female circumcizers,
no acid-hurling avengers of adultery,
no one who speaks of "The Infidels."
I want a moral means test,
a safe haven for all who would resist
the call to tempered steel, *a border,*

for those who do not know where to begin
to defend themselves or their sleepless kin.
Lovely Assia Bayeesh,
enter as a refugee, bring your little cousin.
May this country forever shield your deep-brown eyes from staring
and staring at *it* again.

JERUSALEM EARTHQUAKE

Beneath the dancing feet of a hundred wedding revellers
the floor opens up, and with terrified screams
three stories collapse into one,
captured in what the TV announcer later names
the most horrific wedding video ever made.
Twenty-five crushed to death, scores more injured.

(a fateful choice among banquet halls for a *simchah,*
a contractor who removed a support beam
to open more commercial space?)

"On the edges of the crater," writes reporter Khaled Abu Toameh,
"where survivors grasped their heads,
the round black-topped tables were eerily unscathed,
wine glasses and bottles of mineral water and soda still standing.
One rescuer said they had found the bodies
of an entire family sitting on chairs
around a party table, smashed in the wreckage."

Yet somehow the groom escapes unhurt
and in hospital his 25-year-old bride survives.
Continues Abu Toameh,
"Her white wedding dress, marked with blood,
lay in a black plastic bag next to her bed."
Please tell all the families that I'm sorry.
Please forgive me, she implores.
From the mother of the groom:
Someone must bear the responsibility.
I don't think I will be able to cope with this disaster."

Will ever an Arab again write so tenderly
of the Children of Israel?

On the same day, two bomb attacks from Islamic Jihad
—an "anniversary gift to the Lebanese."
One a bomb-laden truck, kills the driver,
the other marries metal with civilian flesh.
In split seconds the Lord's dominion over the earth
shakes and quavers.

Abu Toameh's closing line rings with irony,
"The family are described by relatives as observant Jews."

INSIDE THIS SCREEN, MY BODY

Intact on an April day when the trees explode in talismans
and the sturdy hornet translates his appetites
into vertigo, hovering outside this wired screen,
my body's crescents anchor an aluminum chair
as I watch faintly steaming joggers lope by
on a charity run,
and though my eyes twitch and blur,
the comforting message is received:
Relax.

Relax and breathe deep on the bounty of denial.
The tendon-bound meat will be unmasked
only should the leg be severed in the dash
or the arm lopped off by a dislodged blade
or other metal artifact in flight.
Far, we are far from Jerusalem
with its unholy flying screws and nails.
Nothing but bad luck rolled into a cancerous ball
can stop the intestine; hollow threats
to this athleticism of tears and strain.

Lowering my eyelids, I hold up my hands at arm's length
like a blind man seeking, offering, benediction:
my two good hands.
Dear lord of the unpredictable,
bless me on this sultry day
for I remain safe and intact
behind my Kevlar screen.

FOOD (FAD)
Guidelines for the New Sobriety

To be the corn-beard, bean-eyed prophet of the working middle class,
an Arcimboldo head of broccoli, carrots, pasta, chicken, fish
and other green, orange and lily-white wholesomes
who swells the cornucopia with *free foods*,
seder-like rituals for the age-old dilemma
what exactly to, not to and never eat,

and how best to help some "fat thin" atone
for a long forefinger's swipe around
the melted remains in the Häagen-Daz container,
where only complex machinery could assemble
so many calories in such a compact space;

Where with the eating comes more than appetite,
comes a horseman,
comes a third buttock,
comes the iceman swinging refills from a long, long pole
straight into the freezers of Pusateri's.

Still the soul wakes groggy from a dream
of pizza toppings steaming with stainless-steel oven heat,
chicken liver/anchovy/ground beef delight,
and the trinity; Napoleon, profiterole, chocolate éclair,
nay, tiramisu!
camping us along the plush pink headboard
we were warned leads only to regression,
an approach to food best classified senatorial,

the inner bulimic crying, "Why does mother keep *bringing*
all this shit into the house?"

But dare I, brought up on giant apple pancakes
& hickory-smoked ham, washed down by finest Colombian
—with respect for any drug from Colombia—
sing the praises of *President's Choice Toasted Os,*
or splashes of *Rose's* lime cordial enhancing
a tall glass of hydrogenated oxygen, rather than rum?
Or long dark colder-than-frozen *Rice Dream* bars,
—or any "free food"?
Dare I, who waited through endless synagogue services
for creamy cheesecakes baked by the Sisterhood,
cakes that resisted the wet knife,

cakes topped with Bing cherries in a scream-red syrup,
shake my finger and do a cosmic "Now, now" or "There, there"
to those slouching back from dietary Bethlehem, with nothing
to show for each rebirth but an extra fifteen pounds?

We need guidelines for the new sobriety,
to defeat the endless mutations in the junk-food armamentarium,
to define the whens and wheres and hows of *safe eating,*
coming up with a diaphragm of principles
to fit antiseptically over the face...

We may yet skirt the abyss of cholesterol,
that insulin-driven gummy-bear paste lining the maws of hell,
to add the extra two to five years,
even as we hide from the sun's death-rays under gooey film
that makes us listless as landed fish
frying in our own sweat,
even as the green-and-white bullet
of psychiatry tops up the sacred serotonin,
dissolving the dreaded mouth hunger,
and restores the blessing of positive relationships,
however propped;
even as we don 3-D glasses in the half-lit boudoir
of the sexual tryst, to see past unshapely shadows,
to couple for that slow rise of heat,
she with the butterfly rash of satisfaction on her chest,
he with that goofy came-again grin,
each remembering the bounty
of a mutual tumescence so miraculous
it eclipses even the puffery
of the golden-brown soufflé.

UNEASY ON THE OPEN FIELD

You lay your dark mane across my chest
and relax me down through a series
of tongue-on-palate manoeuvres,
but I can't open every pore
—you would just take me in
like ambrosia.

Your nerves settled long ago.
For you, no flashbacks of the blue van
that stalked me through childhood
for a promise of sweet surrender.

How steadily we decline.
Perhaps it's those extra babies we will never have,
the blurry march of candles across a chancy cake.
Soon we will have our long stay
at the home for the profound
—orderly, living
one supervised task at a time.

For the troubling now,
small and uneasy on the open field,
I count the stars in the impenetrable sky
as impersonal blows, but settle for the comfort
of your vaporous voice:
"We things of beauty were not meant to last."

MISSING AND PRESUMED

From the cover of the free subway paper,
winsome she beams with eternally glistening hair,
a sixteen-year-old who never was
—an image generated by computer
from the features of the little girl, missing
and presumed slain, ten years ago today.
Captioned "What Nicole might look like now."
Her father is quoted as saying that one morning
he will be pulled from the shower
by the surprise phone call of his life,
reason enough to outwait
this life's worth of tragedy.

Her simulated teenage smile real
as my own daughter's,
how can her father bear to look
on this vanished fruit of his marriage,
this mirage meant to reassure
that Nicole may yet walk among us,
broken free from a killer's grasp,
though, to be accurate,
both weapon and assailant
are missing and presumed.

Also missing: the final clarity
of that moment by the grave
when a father flings a first spadeful of earth
onto a box that contains his own
still-beating heart.

WE KILL THE AFTERNOON

You and I, love, refuse to up the ante
of existence.
We would rather lie dazed
at the foot of this huge revolving rock,
sipping cabernet
and savouring *brioches*.
True, the granite might leave its pirouette
and crush us, at the very least interrupt
our groping, and whispering,
 "What's the point, was there ever a point?..."

Is this just nuclear *chic*
as those with only hard dry bread
might call it?
How much longer can we ignore
the forces that flung us from the adult world,
daring them to land on us again.

THE CAGE DWELLER

The bars once felt substantial,
once made him feel his anger would fall flat,
that trying to break out would be pointless.
Now they undulate,
grow farther apart with his better moods,
heave in and out slowly
as if to consider releasing him.

But on Friday the sun lit up his body
and he discovered there was no escape,
saw exactly where the bars began:
they grew from his own ribs
and where metal met bone
the transition zone was so subtle
that all these years it had eluded him.

Now he couldn't pull on them without feeling breathless,
couldn't pound them without causing raging pain in his chest.
Still, he felt secure that he had pinpointed "Origins"
though he worried they might end in his lower body
as subtly as they began.
At some point along their tortuous course
he might be able to sever them
and still survive.

From outside came suggestions;
one was that he outgrow the bars.
But he wasted no time on the words of "the idle free";
he was used to these bars now
knew exactly how much he could move them,
the cage became
his passionate study.

He decided that patient waiting in silence,
restricting his movements and his breathing
might weaken the bars; he would erode
the very bases of the flesh that supported them!
"Only wise passivity can forestall an early death
and other shocks to this sensible captivity."

THERE IS A FAMILIARITY

There is a familiarity with the bowels known to yogis
and to those half-blind and forgotten in nursing homes
who hover in limbo between intake and output
with little control over either.

Oh, those spaces in the self that are their own reward,
that can be emptied only by acts of irrigation
that may swell and oppress like subcontinental rivers
or balloons inside a skull.

Can the body be trusted?
Too quick to delegate, it refers bowel pain to the ovary,
ovarian pain to the bowel,
in moves more expedient than versatile.

No wonder we struggle to achieve control,
to silence the stomach, to steady the heart and hand,
to project the voice through the skull
for the cathedral resonance of the actor,

making a manta ray of the diaphragm muscle,
pretending mouth and anus are so much further apart
than a body twisted in on itself can provide for,
and always, with the same goal:

>   to strike a rare and precious pose,
>   as a soul—

TOMBSTONE FLICKER

Tombstones are not motionless;
they flicker in dreams,
in videos taken by amateurs,
in ominous X-rays;
they echo in oval clouds
painted by chronics in the back wards
of asylums.

Coffins are not portable;
two women on a picnic blanket
can be lifted with ease,
yet the burden of one dead woman
makes six lovers mourning her strain
with effort.

Graveyards are not homey,
though home to the many dead on this earth,
though on prime city land
and peaceful countryside;
though built, like any home,
of removable wood and intractable stone.

You see:
crushed hopes, shortened futures
condense like a fog
around each weary mourner
who interrupts a busy day
to pay homage
to the great interruption.

Your own heavy sighing
thickens that fog,
drives you from the graveyard
with the same determination
you secretly use
to find your way back in.

TWO WALKS, SAME NIGHT

On this warm wet night
two men, neighbours,
set out on a walk
and talk sports and politics,
gun control, Cuba, Bosnia,

while one street over
two women also converse
in measured cadence
about what sun conditions and variety of soil
will benefit which plants

and where to enroll
their kids
and what in the approaches
of public versus private schools
and a variety of garden exposures
is just right
or exactly wrong
for each of their particular
offshoots.

THE CONSULTANT

FIVE-PATTERN BALDNESS

1.

After the stylist slipped a thick wig
over my eighteen-year-old head,
pressing down the sides
to lessen the *bouffant* of the damn thing,
he remarked, "Of course, you'll need a bathing cap
to protect your new investment on the beach."
"A bathing cap?" I frowned in the mirror.
"You show me a man walking the sand," he said,
"who's wearing a bathing cap
and bet your bottom dollar,
he's either protecting his hairpiece
or, more likely, he's ashamed of a shiny pate."
The wig man's vision of middle age:
every day a bad-hair day
       or, as years later, I saw in a Stratford shop
       an image on a mug of a tousled Shakespeare
       captioned "Bard Hair Day."
       Who dreamed that self-styled smoothies
       would reign as the titans of the NBA?
       —though theirs is but a truce
       in a different kind of war with hair.

2.

As hard-jogging yuppies hurtle towards
the precipice of advanced years,
pressure mounts to find a preventive—a cure—
for mankind's oldest problem.
Some submit to "scalp reduction,"
forfeiting under a general anaesthetic
the forehead lines etched by mortgages, caterers and time.
"Concerned about hair loss? Consult your doctor,"
pitches the salesman, holding up
anti-male-hormone cream
to rub in night and morning.

3.
Men's magazines provide cameo restorations
with glum Before and smiling After mug shots
across from the page where some hulking bozo kicks sand
onto the blanket of a 98-pounder, whose date
squawks, "Are you gonna let him get away with that?"
Turn the page for ads on Ben Weider, at middle age hard as rock,
French love potions and tiny cameras for boys to see around walls,
penis expanders that really work
and a veritable tool shed
of vibrators.

4.
It's testosterone
that makes the hairline beat a hasty retreat
awakening the Yul Brynner/Kojack/Isaac Hayes in us all.
Or rather, a clown-haired, half-mad professor,
mumbling formulae and the sheepish defence,
"No grass grows on a busy street."

5.
From under the balcony of a full opera house
at a *Nutcracker* premiere,
a hundred bald and balding heads
freshly oiled with auditorium heat
wink up in their nakedly personal and unique
language like the masks of cartoon characters,
their expressions beyond their owners' gazes
dead opposite to what they feel.
The similarity of these baldies, the sheer anonymity!
—Not to mention an ever-bald section of self, a stretch
hairless as far back as history,
the retractable, winking Monty Python "one-eyed trouser snake,"
in more biblical times as original as sin,
that whispers, menacing,
Which of those boneheads down there is you?

ENDOCRINOLOGY

Beside me on the subway
a bearded Orthodox figure from my youth
has surfaced as an endocrinologist,
dapper in a black rain hat.

"So what's new and exciting?" I ask.
"Islet cell transplants.
Though it's still very early.
I tell my diabetics: Neil Armstrong walks on the moon,
it's a giant step for mankind, sure. But it's thirty years
before the first tourist can go up. We're a long ways off."
"Hmm. And the kids?"
"So many kids these days have been on steroids,
and there's all these girls with anorexia
—it's an epidemic of bad bones.
'Course, that's all calcium-and-phosphates stuff.
Not a particular interest of mine.
But we have a promising young researcher."

It's time for us to separate.
"Why not drop by a poetry reading one of these days?"
He gives me a knowing smile as he disembarks.
"I'm swamped."
But his eye twitches—not a wink—
and I know I won't see him again
unless one of my children falls ill.

MAN IN A PINSTRIPE MOOD

She mourns efficiently, the good swift cry,
me, I finger a cigarette
like Zeus at the intercom,
the double door of the office shut,
tweed blazer sprawled on the lazy boy,
alone in my vest, and thinking
of a painting by Cézanne:
Boy in a Red Vest
—Michelangelo di Rosa,
a favourite model because,
as the books say,
Cézanne did not trust strangers.

But it's the wife who has gone strange
and hers is the power to leave—
Watch for alimony clouds on the horizon.
A golden cholesterol-tainted tear
from *Dorland's Medical Dictionary*,
pearly, fat-like monatomic alcohol,
knifes down the border of the face. Ow.

A walk to the fiftieth-storey window
looking out over the park,
air full of cinders and rain.
A visit to the restroom, to write on the wall,
Here I sit, broken-hearted.
Gave it the best years of my life,
And only farted.

I can be sullen,
the beached whale
opposing with my weight
and a begrudging ill-timed ambergris.
Love is heavy-handed,
but it can't move me.

Call for my secretary with pool-table legs
hand-picked to appease my wife
after the last horizontal fiasco.
Switch off/ switch the whole damn thing on/off,
loosen the tie, knock back a few,
hit a shrink who owes a favour for a stock tip
for something to help with sleep.

It's the night that causes problems, half the day's fear
is of the dark,
its clammy fingers on the throat.
No office lighting can dispel it,
unrelenting as guilt,
in our case, mild regret.

THE HUMMING FIRE HALL

You accuse me of wanting you morning and noon.
Too fast, you come on too fast, you say.
Or you blow me out of the air
like a torched moth: *Don't make me feel
hassled / hmmmn hmmmn hmmmn*
I am lucky in what I have to do,
to grow fireproof as a hall in flames
while I make you so big in my onion head
that the whole brainy process starts straining
and in-folding.
You know you won't kill me easily.
I hope you know; do you?
What are you banking on?
A tail-eating exit? A sense of humor
behind a reflex gag?
I am as much a joke as a hassle to anyone:
my despair has the Human Relations people
depressed-but-calm
though the fire hall is humming
like never before...

TAMMY WYNETTE

Thought by some to be a whiner
she stood by five separate men
and endured the heat of house fires,
a kidnapping and torrents of dumb rage.

Now of blessed memory,
her soul pours from the stereo
even as her body double is strapped in
beside thick-wristed young entrepreneurs
who race their sport utilities on Friday nights
up to Richmond Hill, where lap-dancing is legal,
and massage parlours offer a quick "rub 'n tug,"
and for a few extra bucks, a "reverse"
and more, if you bring your own
protection.

For these who transform the matrimonial flesh
to pale plaster, it's "the next best thing to mutuality
—when you're cut back to once-a-week
by a pregnant-looking princess
with a cottage-cheese ass
who only uses her painted lips
to blow kisses at her father."

HARLEQUINS

I have a pill good enough
to get me through the day whole,
another to tame the stomach and bowel,
a third to hoist me fearless on a soapbox,
and a fourth to keep me safe
from the allure of cigarettes and gin.
Multicoloured harlequins throw a shroud over buzzing thought,
and deliver a swift escape into dreamless sleep.

My favourite is half pink, half blue,
relaxing just to look at you
winking, shimmering
on the enamel ledge.
The swallowing can be risky,
or precious: a fallen messenger retrieved
from the floor or the edge of a drain in the sink.
True, the masking can wear off early
or cloud the senses long past dawn.
        But who in this earthly comedy is perfect?
        I was born with a double hernia, tonsils that were colonized,
        an appendix that dropped, and a cyst in my neck
        which the surgeons hunted for in vain.

Catch them at their next opening,
the Medicine Cabinet Door,
bright as candy in their plastic cases,
more play-makers than scientific specimens:
breakfast, lunch and dinner doses,
all lined up and waiting with sunshiny faces.
Some accompany on overnights
in narrow child-proof vials,
some I dare not name aloud
lest the world smile that smile
and slowly twirl a finger 'round its ear.
None are like those streetwise boffoes, Coke and Weed
or that twisted Alphabet gang, E, LSD and K
that punch holes in the senses
and leave me in a ditch for days.
Yet these friends from the pharmacy
also speed up or slow down time.
Though it may dry the nose and mouth and make the eyes blur,
there's a certain certified something for each and every man
if only he can swallow her.

LAST CALL

"Sometimes it seems this hobbling through life without skin
agitated or sunk by each rise and fall of the seasonal sun
is no life calling.
Responsiveness is bad for the arteries.

Let Hank Gorecki write Symphony No. 3 for us all.
He has my sympathy.
Let no one miss the days before we stopped caring
who's sleeping on top of which city grate,
or in whose purloined bed.

Damned if I'll lie down with the daisies
while the surface-skimmers of Big Business whiz by
in cocaine-and-Viagra-fired Land Rovers
decked with cell phones and four-wheel drive,
pulling free of everyone's pain,
with far too little of their own.

What's the hidden message in that Jim Carrey film *The Mask?*
In the end it's about borrowed bravura
you can keep just till sunset, or is it six months
before you revert to a sickly pumpkin-faced man
with sloppily carved eyes and a lining
of thick, candle-singed mush.

Far better to be Jack the Pumpkin King
humming contrapuntally against the plaintive flow of Gorecki's Symphony,
Hey-diddly-dee, the Prozac life for me!"

THE OLD CARDIOLOGY DREAM

Last night I had
the old cardiology dream,
of a baby born with six hearts.
So many valves that could falter!
And how rare,
the necessary synchrony.

Baby, I will cherish you,
one-man percussion band that you are,
and devote my life
to seeing yours through.
May none of your frail pink hearts
break mine.

BUTTONS SLEEPING

Lying beside Buttons, frisky
tricolour Sheltie, admiring her half-lidded sleep,
tan snout, small black nostrils drawing air,
downy rib cage silently expanding.
Against my hand,
I can feel a gentle drumming of heart valves, closer
than a sleeping wife would welcome,
and not a quiver of lust.
Slowly she licks her lips.
Is she dreaming of a Milkbone
or of tonguing a salmon tin?
Not without risk, this *coeur à coeur*.
I may be dubbed an animal lover,
be obliged to go vegetarian,
or finance hip replacements
for her final three years.
I stroke her shield of fleecy white,
and whisper, "You're just a dog,"
and remember a book of poems
called *The Day the Dog Smiled*.
But once again the surreal remains dormant.
For now, at least, she's not frantically chasing
a game of snooker, barking shrilly
at those gleaming unreachable spheres
with their loud rhythmic smacks
and perfunctory pocket drops.
Only this: a steady circling of my heart
with the baffling, regular rhythm
of her own.

ELEPHANT STREET

A FATEFUL RENDERING
New Year's Eve, 2000

To strains of "auld lang syne," the computers are crying,
hooked in train, they thrum in their giant hangar,
churning frames for a blockbuster animation.
Night shift on the "rendering farm."

He inhales the vapours of a dozen vats of ink,
a smell like copy-machine toner that awakens the bowel,
reminding him of his own frail animation,
—not the lean six-foot frame or the quickening heart that moves it

but rather, this work-in-progress, his one-computer
tribute to Osip Mandelstam,
the Russian-Jewish poet exiled
to death in his thirties by Stalin.

The sole image: a red flag waving
but *briskly* despite the total stillness of the day
as a solitary line of poetry
flickers into view.

The slightest interruption of power could kill the project,
or send it back to its starting point.
Once completed, and copied onto CDs, he will hand it to friends
to run at a few set times, and together think of Mandelstam.

"You're a hard guy to categorize,"
said a biographer friend, intending a compliment.
"It's a noble gesture, but what's your point?
Where's the remuneration?"

He could only answer, "I like being a question mark.
I don't have the pluck of a Mandelstam
who ran off from the police station clutching a sheaf
of trumped-up warrants-for-arrest of his artist friends."

The clock edges past midnight in the beam of a thousand machines
plowing on, oblivious as sheep. "Two thousand and *one*.
All right, then, the twenty-*first* century."
I will enter the coming age it seems, but I will not see it coming.

TEMPORARY POWER

He graded my office: "Commanding window,
far from the washrooms… nice, very nice,"
and, after years of working together, he offered a transference dream:
"I was flying over jagged cliffs, but with the aid of a minor device."
"To what do you associate this?"
"I don't know," he said, looking me over, "perhaps a microchip."

Sometimes—never at once—we tasted the lakes
of each other's eyes, he assessing, me admiring;
his stunning looks distracting a professional drive
to shore up his flimsy ego. I longed to help him,
though sick of how coldly he spoke of his fiancée.
I thought of the recent "brown-outs" in Silicon Valley—
and British Columbia helping out with temporary power.

He wore his American ambition like a flag, at times a Confederate flag
that warned of a colossal hurt pride. Things he carried:
The Wall Street Journal, Fortune, Forbes and *Vanity Fair.*
He parked his SUV "truck" in two of the clinic's parking spaces.
He drank only filtered water, the parched landscape of his casino-like past
fueled a need to sink pipelines into the terrain of other lives,
impetuously laid and manned by sentries.
Evenings he said the high-tech rosary,
Microsoft, Intel, Cisco and *Oracle,*
and cursed bitterly when the bubble burst and his margins were called.

Words like *wuss* and *wimp* tripped freely from his lips and stoked the fires
of self-hatred. His dark suits were centered by silk ties of deep red and navy blue
that switched on brooding-firmament eyes.
He held fast to his parents' hypochondria and had "no use for fiction
any more than for self-help."
I served him in his empire for as long as I was needed, swept aside
by a change of heart, or was it regime?
Years later he described me as kindly, very *Canadian.*

PAINT-CAN HERO

fuddy-duddy-didi-do.

That's how he hears my sober advice about police stings and blindness and
tours of the burn ward for those who wind up downwind from flaming plumes
of aerosol.

"Whadda you know about highs? *You* ever tag a truck or a train
or kill a wall or a GAP billboard or feel the rush when those idiots from
        Security close in,
neither of 'em expecting you to turn on them with pepper spray?
You ever smell the sizzlin' root beer you get when you blow brown paint
through a lighter or redo a subway ad with a wax stick that takes *years* to remove?
Believe me, I know the scene: A train engineer caught me and my buddy
in the act and told us, Wait, guys, till I park the train further down the track,
then it won't be on my watch."

He gets me thinking. We've been meeting for a year
yet he sneers as he plunks a slick magazine on graffiti art on my coffee table.
Who publishes this? Who *was* that engineer?
A disgruntled employee, pandering to young blood—or a patron
of the arts from the other side of the tracks?

THE FOLEY ARTIST

A rare professional who manufactures sounds
for the off-mike action
to mix into the final version of a film.
He may squeeze a bag of baking soda for footsteps
or tiptoe across open bins of earth, sand and gravel
to match his tread with that of the skulking actor on the screen.
Tricks get played, but are only economically cheap:
an upchuck of vomit translates to wads of soaked kleenex
flopped into a metal pan, a rustle of roaches' wings,
even the mouthings of a lizard are rendered
by thin splinters of balsa wood ground gently together
inside or outside a jar.
A sloppy pulling at the side of the cheek in a *sgoosh-sgoosh*
denotes a frantic sexual solo.
The beating of a supermarket chicken, bones crunching,
electrifies the final boxing round.
A second's work, to the foley artist: the screech of nails
on a backboard, in harmony with the sudden arc
of a teacher's chalk.

No foley artist, the stereotype Rogerian
who echoes back his patient's every intent:
"What I hear you saying is you're feeling depressed;
if I hear you right, you're feeling *very* depressed;
you say you're so depressed you're about to jump out my window."
And, as the patient leaps,
the wistful Rogerian approaches the window,
looks down the forty-storey drop,
and, in detached synchrony, whispers, "Plop."

No foley artist, the "fence-hopper" peeping Tom,
reassured rather than panicked at the sight of a naked man,
knowing the man's naked lover (or his porno)
will soon emerge into view,
he too fills in the soundtrack.
Nor should such a devotee of silent viewing be confused
with a drunken teenage cow-tipper, breaker of night silence
who thrives on an unlikely thud and startled *moooo*!
to shatter the night's peace and reignite his sense of agency.

I would be your foley artist, give sound
to the sequences of a childhood where screams were silenced
by the muffling hand of dissociation.
I offer a score in which no phantom can brush your cheek

without a cottony forewarning, no assailant creep up
on your children with a stalker's noiseless tread.
For now I keep these bins filled
with earth, water, air and fire.
I take my lead from apparitions
in your silent dreams.

RIFFS ON DIGNITY

I have my own list, though it's jumbled and merely personal.

Chick Webb was the Toulouse-Lautrec of the jazz world,
straining past his painful deformity to keep pace
with Benny Goodman and Count Basie at the Savoy.
"Pub" is an eloquent labour lawyer with polio:
the friend who braved operations on both his feet
in the hope of walking like the man he is but cannot be.
—Then there's a young freshman
who transcends a large tumour behind her eye
turning it into merely a sightless hillock
by refusing to miss a single class.
I think sometimes of Tracy Latimer,
disabled, deformed, dismembered by repeated surgery,
a Saskatchewan farm girl put to sleep by her own dad
as the loner in the herd not meant to make it.
I pass others on the street,
with the "upper motor neuron lesions"
that make them spastic, and hear
their determined slapping riffs on dignity.

I squinted through the clouds of carbon monoxide
pouring from the mouth of mercy rigged to a tailpipe,
and had a vision:

My own slender corpse washes up on a rock,
at the lake, after a solo swim in the bracing water,
reduced —elevated?—to lake-turtle status,
hands clenched double, Joe Cocker-style,
on my face the old *rictus sardonicus*
as from the side of my bearded mouth
they squeeze water, then air,
then a final attempt at a drinking song.
Drying me out under the warm lamps
the nurse brings e-mailed photos of loved ones, books to console,
a chaplain to insist that "others bear their suffering, their plight
can enlarge the soul if only you allow them in."
Through the long night each holds up a mirror, should I suddenly awaken.
They need me to do more than add myself to a list
which is jumbled and merely personal.
They conspire in their silence, they insist
 I fill out the corpus of my work.

BLUE SPERM WHALE

His patient brings in a dream,
to infiltrate his own:
I'm about five, I'm on a windy beach
dragging at the sand with my hands,
when suddenly, I bring into view
the rubbery brow of some long-submerged ocean beast.
My fingernails keep clawing, clawing
aching from the pressure,
till after what feels like hours
I unearth its entire body:
A blue sperm whale.
Is it alive?

Cautiously, he interprets
her painful struggle to expose
yet somehow contain an old Oedipal menace.
Now, after five years on his taut leather couch,
on a morning in late April,
she sits up and confesses, *I love you.*

Other images she shared
speed through his mind:
her mother's horrified scream
when she walked in on them
and her father urgently covered his naked wife,
vague memories of the thrashing that followed,
her back and neck lashed
with the pain of barbed ocean waves
and a terrible excitement.
Now, crowning up through the sand
shamelessly naked and blue,
this spent beast from the sea
and more, *I love you.*

He recalls that her dreams are often
mined with fish hooks. Here too,
Each time I try to free their grips
they snare and bite at my fingers.
Mentors from his training
circle like pilot fish,
offering a school of evasive replies
from a feeble "I too have feelings for you,"
to a simple, suspect "Thank you,"

as if he were gaining, no, maintaining
an upper hand, as in the lament:
The patient has a vantage point,
the therapist an advantage point.

I love you too, trips off his lips
because of the truth,
because the risk of losing his licence
seems banal against her gallery of ocean images.
And though he knows she has been raped
and repeatedly mistreated,
(The Rapist, she nicknamed a doctor from her past,)
he rises from his chair as she rises from his couch
for a long silent hug.

Later he tells a frowning colleague
who specializes in physician abuse,
"Hugging a female patient is never sexual
for me; it only happens from the waist up."

But even as he defends his stance
he senses the stirring head of a blue sperm whale
desperate to free itself from the sand.
A nearby buoy shines bright as a cenotaph.
Stretched across the excavated pit
where once a whale tried to surface,
he grieves what little remains, lines of tiny barbs
glistening, twitching in the ocean breeze,
painted with freshly drawn blood.

ELEPHANT STREET

for those who chart the red shift of galaxies

When Israel went forth from Egypt, Armand and I
wound our way through another spring.
The Jordan turned back a rush of hot-dog smells,
a pollen of street dust and car stereos blasting through open windows.
The mountains skipped like rams past panhandlers and boutiques,
and Armand grinned down at me like a carnivorous fish.
"Judaism is an aesthetic choice," he said. *The sea saw it and fled.*

An expanding universe is speeding up. My step slows.
I had shaken my head: "How can anyone be an atheist?"
"But *you're* an atheist," he thunders over the busy intersection.
"There are *hundreds* of Gods you don't believe in
—the elephant-headed Ganesh— and only *one* in which you do."
We're in for a lovers' quarrel.

I scoured the universe with questions, scrubbing until it was nearly clean,
but by the Gates of Prayer we stopped again to dodge the cars.
Half-heartedly, I switched back to science,
the "eternal molecules" argument, which he side-swiped.
"If a car were to hit you between here and Spadina Avenue,
would your family be consoled
to know your molecules were still here?
You wouldn't be forgotten, but you'd be gone."
The heavens belong to the Lord, but the earth is given to mortals.
That made me look around and count
the number of streets on which a Jew could walk.

A universe was speeding up when it should slow down.
We parted the seas, as usual, on good terms.
The rock of his heart by then must have been turning to water;
we are just flints from which sparks are struck.
It is not the dead who praise the Lord, it is not those who go down to silence.

It's like that, talking about God over lunch hour
as the seasons change on the unforgiving concrete.
"To Fate," Armand calls back a final time,
raising an imaginary wine glass as he steps into traffic,
"no matter how we render it."

EPILOGUE

AT THE ROANOKE

Senatorial, with black eyebrows under a shock of white hair,
Uncle Maurice calls The Roanoke
"this cruise ship of a retirement home."
It features six restaurants, each with an escalating dress code.
Since I wear neither jacket nor tie,
we head off the central foyer
for the least pricey dining room
—the one best lit for Maurice
who, despite a sagacious stare, is legally blind.
In lieu of umbrellas and overcoats,
diners check walkers and canes at the door.
Parkinsonian men in Lacoste sportswear
shuffle to seats or jam to a stop
where marble flooring meets hardwood.

Around us, dark oak wainscotting
cedes to sun-bleached walls of Florida marl.
Above our heads, on the mezzanine,
faux-limestone balustrade pillars
too closely spaced to be classical
are designed to prevent losses
of a great-grandchild or an ivory-headed cane.

Maurice nods toward the far wall:
"Death is just on the other side,
but these walls are reinforced
to block out the beeps from Intensive Care.
I know, from the way it was touch and go last week."

He means the misadventures that convinced him
to buy into The Roanoke:
a thyroid tumor that turned out to be huge,
its removal fraught with complications,
how tidepools of bright blood oozed
from a Foley catheter mistakenly inserted into the space
where he once had a prostate.
How sending him home to recuperate nearly killed him.

The diners sip steaming soup,
some wearing nasal prongs,
and a paralyzed man in an ascot with an electric board

punches out his menu choices.
"The indignities of growing old," I comment.
"Best to check your dignity at the door."

He adds, "I don't care to think
of being here twenty years from now,
but you always want that next day,"
a more sanguine way to put it, in my view,
than "take it one day at a time."
He's the great rationalist in our family,
our last holdout from spirituality.
His "God" is nothing more than "Good Odds."
A few years ago he toured Europe's cathedrals
for the sake of his late Christian wife,
and he called those architectural *stupendi*
"God-boxes" in her hearing.

"Quite a place you have here, Uncle." I note
the blonde South African waitress,
both fetching and formal, and ever attentive
to the needs of necessity's picky eaters.
"Yes, this is quite the place,"
though in all the restaurants, he confides,
the meals are pretty much the same;
only the décor and lighting change
in a world of low-sodium veal marsala.

 "After supper I'll show you the dollhouses upstairs
and the train set in Santa's village
and these strange Victorian shadowbox rooms
where dolls do needlepoint in formal wear
on tiny balsa rocking chairs. It's eerie,
just this side of kitsch,
but it's all built by residents,
and their grandchildren love it.
The shingles of the general store
are really tongue depressors, laid
by the widowed pediatrician down the hall.

"Two more weeks of this,
and I may give up my opposition
to the death penalty," he winks,
again nodding at that far wall
towards which an air-bagged fresh recruit
is now quietly being wheeled.
"That's the closest you get to 'the bum's rush'
here at The Roanoke."

THE NIGHT AFTER

The night after I learned
they uncovered a plan to dynamite the daycare centre
I reached back in time
for my frail infant son
swaddling-blanketed following ritual circumcision,
and when I found him, I lowered him
into the snow-covered earth of Canada,
then withdrew him, to consecrate
—if the world would allow it—
the life he would lead as a Jewish man
with newborns of his own.

But now the matter rests in Security's poorly paid hands,
and in the Middle East the judgement hour advances
so swiftly that even talk
about "a two-state solution,"
about "building first the wall, then making the peace,"
about "post-Zionism," and forcing both sides to relocate,
—all the talk on this Earth cannot dampen my fear
of a world bereft of holiness.

Like benediction, relief comes
only from immersion in sleep
and in earth yet unclaimed
by a long-forgotten dream of peace,
a peace that stretches not just from Cairo to Amman
but Baghdad to Riyadh, Beirut to Damascus
—to Jerusalem! —
all the sacred incendiary points between
Salaam and *Shalom.*

ABOUT THE AUTHOR

Ron Charach was born and raised in Winnipeg, and educated in medicine and psychiatry in Winnipeg, Toronto and New York, completing his training in child and adolescent psychiatry at The New York Hospital-Cornell Medical Center in 1980. His poetry has appeared in most Canadian literary journals, as well as in the *Lancet* and *The New England Journal of Medicine,* and in the anthology of world physician poetry, *Blood & Bone,* published by the University of Iowa Press. Ron Charach's poems have won praise from prize-winning poets as diverse as Roo Borson, Don Coles and Don McKay.

POETRY COLLECTIONS
BY RON CHARACH

The Big Life Painting

The Naked Physician
(Anthology)
*Poems about the Lives of
Patients and Doctors*

Someone Else's Memoirs

Past Wildflowers

Petrushkin!

Dungenessque

AGMV Marquis

MEMBRE DE SCABRINI MEDIA

Québec, Canada
2003